DEVELOPING THE MAN IN THE MIRROR

DEVELOPING THE MAN IN THE MIRROR

Rufus M. Parker

Developing the Man in the Mirror

by Rufus M. Parker

©Copyright 2002 Word Aflame Press
Hazelwood, MO 63042-2299

Cover photography and design by Paul Povolni

ISBN 1-56722-583-7

The following references were used: The Thompson Chain Reference Bible, Fifth Edition, King James Version; 1988; Lincoln on Leadership, Donald T. Phillips, Warner Books; 1992; The Founding Fathers on Leadership, Donald T. Phillips, Warner Books; 1997; Military Leadership; FM 22-100; Department of the Army; July 1990; Distribution Restriction: Approved for Public Release; Distribution is Unlimited; The Noncommissioned Officers Guide; TC 22-6; Headquarters Department of the Army; November 1990; Distribution Restriction: Approved for Public Release; Distribution is Unlimited; Leadership How To; FORSCOM Pamphlet 600-7; January 1989; Local Exact reproduction authorized.

Printed in United States of America.

WORD AFLAME®PRESS
8855 DUNN ROAD
HAZELWOOD, MO 63042-2299

CONTENTS

NOTABLE QUOTES

"Leadership is intangible, and therefore no weapon ever designed can replace it."

—General Omar Bradley

"If anything goes bad, then I did it. If anything goes semi-good, then we did it. If anything goes real good, then you did it."

—William Cullen Bryant

"There is no limit to what can be accomplished if it doesn't matter who gets the credit."

—Ralph Waldo Emerson

"Don't lose confidence in your people when they fail."
"If you practice dictatorial leadership, you prepare yourself to be dictated to."
"Remember, the best leaders never stop learning."
"His cardinal mistake is that he isolated himself, & allows nobody to see him; and by which he does not know what is going on in the very matter he is dealing with."

—The president's reason for relieving General John C. Fremont from his command in Missouri (September 9, 1861)

—Abraham Lincoln

"If you think you are indispensable, you ain't."

"Wars may be fought by weapons, but they will be won by men. It is the spirit of the men who follow and the men who lead that gains victory."

"Never tell people how to do things. Tell them what needs to be done, and they will surprise you with their ingenuity."

"All men are frightened. The more intelligent they are, the more they are frightened. The courageous man is the man who forces himself, in spite of his fear, to carry on."

—*General George S. Patton*

"If you treat a man as he is, he will remain as he is. If you treat him as if he were what he could be and should be, he will become what he could be and should be."

—*Johann Wolfgang Von Goethe*

"We must make the best of mankind as they are, since we cannot have them as we wish."

"To be prepared for war is one of the most effectual means of preserving peace."

—*General George Washington*

"Discipline is doing the right thing when no one is watching you."

—*Command Sergeant Major Rufus M. Parker*

PREFACE

This book is not written as some other leadership books you may have read in the past. Its purpose is to cause you, the leader, to focus on making yourself a better leader.

For over twenty-eight years in the military, I was instructed in the ways of leadership. I was given many opportunities to fail so that I might one day become a good leader. This is one way the Army develops its leaders. Being forced to adhere to the Noncommissioned Officers' (NCO) Creed pushed me to focus on my daily responsibilities as a leader. The Army demands outstanding leadership from all of its officers and NCOs. Those who are unwilling to take the challenge will soon find themselves left in the dirt or demoted for inefficiency.

The NCO Education System (NCOES) is just one of the professional training institutes that the Army has for developing leaders. If someone reaches the level of attending and graduating from the Sergeant Majors Academy, he has been taught leadership at every level and is capable of functioning in any leadership position that the military has to offer.

People must realize that leaders are not born; they are made. Leadership development must be an integral part of every leader's agenda, and he must also have a plan for developing new leaders.

Leadership often involves parenting. The organization is the family, and the leader is the head of the family. Therefore, leaders must guide and nurture the people under them the same way that parents nurture their own children. As children will take on the nature and character of the leader of the home, so the organization will take on the personality of its top leader. If you are a good leader, when your work is done and your aim is fulfilled, your people will say, "We did this ourselves."

When Jesus called Simon Peter and his brother Andrew, He said, "Follow me, and I will make you fishers of men" (Matthew 4:18-19). This is a case in point of leadership development. Leaders should strive to develop and train people to assume responsibility in the event that something happens to their leader.

The greatest reference for developing leaders is the Word of God.

The greatest reference for developing leaders is the Word of God. It has everything: problem solving, dealing with difficult people, counseling, handling the complex and difficult situations that the leader may encounter, etc. Jesus Christ is the ultimate leader—yesterday, today, and forever.

Being a leader is not hard if you apply the following biblical principles:

- Treat others as you would have them treat you (Matthew 7:12).
- Love others like Jesus loves you (John 15:12).
- Obey and submit to your leaders (Hebrews 13:17).
- Give honor to whom honor is due (Romans 13:7).
- Live peacefully with all people (Romans 12:18).
- God shows partiality to no one; neither should you (Acts 10:34).
- Love your neighbor as yourself (Matthew 22:39).
- Seek first the kingdom of God (Matthew 6:33).
- Be wise as a serpent and harmless as a dove (Matthew 10:16).

In addition to the principles above, I would add: Do the right thing when no one is watching you.

LEADERSHIP
DEFINED

Leadership is the art of influencing and directing people in such a way as to gain their willing obedience, loyalty, and confidence to accomplish the mission.

NONCOMMISSIONED OFFICERS' CREED

"No one is more professional than I. I am a Non-commissioned Officer, a leader of soldiers. As a Noncommissioned Officer, I realize that I am a member of a time-honored corps, which is known as 'The Backbone of the Army.'

"I am proud of the Corps of Noncommissioned Officers and will at all times conduct myself so as to bring credit upon the Corps, the Military Service and my country regardless of the situation in which I find myself. I will not use my grade or position to attain pleasure, profit, or personal safety.

"Competence is my watchword. My two basic responsibilities will always be uppermost in my mind—accomplishment of my mission and the welfare of my soldiers. I will strive to remain tactically and technically proficient. I am aware of my role as a Noncommissioned Officer. I will fulfill my responsibilities inherent in that role. All soldiers are entitled to outstanding leadership; I will provide that leadership. I know my soldiers and will always place their needs above my own. I will communicate consistently with my soldiers and never leave them uninformed. I will be fair and impartial when recommending both reward and punishment.

"Officers of my unit will have maximum time to accomplish their duties; they will not have to accomplish mine. I will earn their respect and confidence as well as that of my soldiers. I will be loyal to those with whom I serve; seniors, peers and subordinates alike. I will exercise initiative by taking appropriate action in the absence of orders. I will not compromise my integrity, nor my moral courage. I will not forget, nor will I allow my comrades to forget that we are professionals, Noncommissioned Officers, **leaders!**"

LEADERSHIP

Leadership is simply the art of *influencing* and *directing* people in such a way as to gain their willing obedience, confidence, and loyalty to accomplish the mission. For over twenty-five of my twenty-eight-year military career, I lived by the creed of the Noncommissioned Officer. Entwined within these words is everything a leader must be, know, and do. It is the cornerstone by which all NCOs in the US Army must live. An NCO is a leader. As a Noncommissioned Officer, I reviewed this creed daily to ensure I was living up to its standards. If the military requires its leaders to live up to a certain standard, shouldn't we as Christians live up to the standards outlined in the Word of God?

The creed is broken into three sections: Professionalism, Competence, and Loyalty. The first section, Professionalism, reminds me that I am a professional, a leader of soldiers, and a part of something that is very important—the backbone of the US Army. We all know that the backbone is the foundation, or the sturdiest part, of the body. In the natural, if you break or damage your backbone (spine), you are not going very far. Therefore, as a leader, I must not do anything that will bring discredit upon myself or other leaders with whom I am associated, regardless of the situation in which I may find myself. The Bible says, "If the foundations be destroyed, what can the righteous do?" (Psalm 11:3).

Now let's look at this from a Christian standpoint. The apostle Paul explained it best: "There is therefore now no condemnation to them which are in Christ Jesus, who walk not after the flesh, but after the Spirit" (Romans 8:1). In other words, there is no blame, denunciation, criticism, reproach, or accusation against them. It's usually when we follow the flesh that we bring discredit upon the organization and ourselves.

The second section of the creed, Competence, reminds me that I must never stop learning. I must possess the skills, knowledge, and abilities to do my job and to be effective. In a sense the apostle Paul drove the nail home when he said, "Till I come, give attendance to reading, to exhortation, to doctrine" (I Timothy 4:13) and "Study to shew thyself approved unto God, a workman that needeth not to be ashamed, rightly dividing the word of truth" (II Timothy 2:15). These scriptures stress that we must become competent.

18

As a leader, I must be aware of my two basic responsibilities. They must always be uppermost in my mind. They are (1) accomplishing the mission and (2) assuring the welfare of the people. As a leader, you must realize the importance of this statement. You cannot accomplish the mission without the people whom God has entrusted to you. An old saying in the military is: "If you take care of the people, they will take care of you." This section of the creed also states, "All soldiers are entitled to outstanding leadership." You may ask why I used the word *soldiers*. Paul said, "No man that warreth entangleth himself with the affairs of this life; that he may please him who hath chosen him to be a soldier" (II Timothy 2:4).

We can't have just any old type of leadership; we must strive for outstanding leadership. Outstanding leadership sets a positive example for others, causing them to emulate it and to be motivated, and makes people want to be a part of the team. When this type of leadership is provided, communication is enhanced between you and the people, and there is no prejudice or unfair treatment of those under your care. In the military, this is called "Seeing Green." Everyone is the same.

The third section of the creed, Loyalty, talks about what it means to be loyal. It says, "The officers over me will not have to do my job." In the Army one of the things I disliked most was encountering an officer having to do an NCO's job or having to

19

remind him what his job was. Our leaders over us should never have to do our job for us. James said, "[He] that knoweth to do good, and doeth it not, to him it is sin" (James 4:17). If those over us cannot trust us to do our job, then we will not earn their respect as a good leader, which again brings discredit upon us and those who have gone before us. The writer of Hebrews said, "Obey them that have the rule over you, and submit yourselves: for they watch for your souls, as they that must give account, that they may do it with joy, and not with grief: for that is unprofitable for you" (Hebrews 13:17). Everyone has a leader—if you don't follow your leader, then those whom you lead will never follow you. A part of following is doing the task assigned to you.

Review the NCO creed and let it become a part of your life, not from a military standpoint, but from a leader's standpoint. You will see the difference it will make in your life.

FACTORS OF LEADERSHIP

o The Led

o The Leader

o The Situation

o Communication

The four factors of leadership should always be in your mind and should always guide the actions you take and when you take them. These four factors are: *The Led, The Leader, The Situation,* and *Communication.*

You must create a climate that encourages your people to actively participate and causes them to want to be a part of accomplishing the mission.

The first major factor is *The Led*—the people under your care and responsibility. All people cannot be led the same way. As a leader you have to know the abilities of the people you are leading. A person given a new job may require closer supervision than others who have done the job before. Some people have very low self-confidence and will need your support and encouragement. A person who works hard and does what he knows to do deserves your praise. The one who knows to do right and doesn't do it needs to be reprimanded.

As a leader you must assess your people's competence, motivation, and commitment so that you can take the correct leadership actions at the correct time. You must create a climate that encourages your people to actively participate and causes them to want to be a part of accomplishing the mission. Key ingredients to developing this relationship are mutual trust, respect, and confidence.

The second major factor is you—*The Leader.* You must have an honest understanding of who you are, what you know, and what you can do. Abraham Lincoln stated, "You can fool some of the people some of the time, but you can't fool all the people all the time." You must know your strengths, weaknesses, capabilities, and limitations so that you can control and discipline yourself and lead effectively. Sometimes it is easier to assess others than yourself. If you have difficulty assessing yourself, ask *your* leader for an honest assessment. Don't put him on the spot. Do it at a time when you are alone together.

As a leader, you have to know yourself and be yourself. I can remember the first time I was asked to preach. I did everything I thought was right as far as preparing my message, but when I went to deliver it, I tried to preach like my pastor instead of being myself. Needless to say I made a mess of it. I knew who I was, but I was trying to be someone else. This will never work as a leader. Be yourself and seek self-improvement.

The third factor of leadership is *The Situation.* All situations are different. The type of leadership that works in one situation may not work in another. In one situation you may have to closely supervise and direct people. Another situation may require you to encourage and listen to their ideas.

The situation also includes the timing of actions. For example, confronting a person may be the correct action, but if the confrontation occurs too soon or too late, the results may not be effective. Have you ever wondered how many times Jesus had seen those merchants and sellers in the Temple before He reacted the way He did? Jesus' example shows us that there is a time for correction. It also shows us that sometimes as a leader you will have to be forceful to get your point across. It doesn't mean that you are ever rude or out of control; it simply means that some things will not be tolerated.

Effective communication occurs when your people understand what you are trying to tell them and when you understand what they are trying to tell you.

What if you take a wrong action? It happens. We all make mistakes. Analyze the situation again, take corrective action, and move on. Learn from your mistakes and from those of others.

The fourth factor of leadership is *Communication*—the exchange of information and ideas from one person to another. Effective communication occurs when your people understand what you are trying to tell them and when you understand what they are trying to tell you. You must realize that you

24

communicate standards by your example as well as by what behaviors you ignore, reward, and punish. Remember, communication is always a two-way street—up and down.

The way you communicate in different situations is important. Your choice of words, tone of voice, and physical actions combine to impact people. Leadership is more than setting the example and leading. Having the ability to say the correct thing at the appropriate moment and in the right way is also an important part of leadership.

Listening is an important part of communication. Remember, if you listen to people, they will listen to you. There is a saying, "I know you think you heard what I said, but I don't think you understood what I meant." Effective communication will insure the message is clear and understood. (In another chapter, we will discuss how to communicate.)

Here is an example of how communications can become misconstrued. I read this in an Army handout.

OPERATION HALEY'S COMET

The colonel told the captain that Haley's Comet would be passing through the area and that he wanted all soldiers in the theater at 0900 Friday so that he could explain this phenomenal event.

The captain called the lieutenant in and informed him that Haley's Comet was going to be passing by the theater on Friday at 0900 and that the colonel wanted all the soldiers available in the theater so that he could explain this phenomenal event.

The lieutenant told the sergeant that General Haley and the colonel would be passing by the theater in a Comet at 0900 on Friday and that all the soldiers should be standing by the theater when they passed so as not to miss this phenomenal event.

The sergeant told the soldiers that General Haley Comet and the colonel were going to be passing through the area on Friday around 0900 hours and that they all needed to be standing by in fatigues to observe this phenomenal event.

This is a prime example of how miscommunication can happen.

Don't think that you are superman. Know who you are and strive to better yourself. Lead your people from the front in a positive manner. Communicate with them. Don't wait until there is a problem to communicate with *The Led.* Establish effective communication when they are on the mountaintop, and they will be prepared to listen to their leader when they are having difficulties.

Don't think that you are superman.

EXPECTATIONS OF A LEADER

o Demonstrate Technical Competence

o Teach Subordinates

o Be a Good Listener

o Treat People with Dignity and Respect

o Stress and Enforce the Basics

o Set the Example

o Set and Enforce Standards

As a leader, you must learn to fulfill both the expectations of those you lead and of other leaders.

Expectations are what people think that you should be, know, and do.

Expectations are what people think that you should be, know, and do. Earlier, I stated that the creed of a Noncommissioned Officer provided me with what I must be, know, and do as a leader. As you review these expectations, ask yourself: "Am I fulfilling the expectations required of me?"

DEMONSTRATE TECHNICAL COMPETENCE

Know your business. Again, the apostle Paul stated, "Study to shew thyself approved unto God, a workman that needeth not to be ashamed, rightly dividing the word of truth" (II Timothy 2:15). The people under you expect you to be competent. As a leader, competency is my watchword.

A competent person understands his job and what is expected of him. He strives to improve in every area of his life. He studies history and what has affected the course of this world. He keeps abreast of current events. He tries to master areas that will help him to be an effective leader and to accomplish his mission. People want to follow people who are confident in their own abilities. The military taught me that there are nine competencies that provide the framework for leadership development and assessment. They estab-

lish broad categories of skills, knowledge, and attitudes that define a leader's behavior. They are:

1. *Technical Proficiency:* You must know your
   job and be able to train others. You must possess the knowledge required to perform all
   functions related to your position, including
   the ability to operate equipment.

2. *Decision Making:* This refers to the skills you
   need in order to make choices and to solve
   problems. Decisions must be made at the low-
   est level of the organization. Decision-making
   is an excellent way to develop your leadership
   team. Your people will observe how you
   respond to different situations and will learn
   from your example.

3. *Planning:* This involves forecasting, setting
   goals and objectives, developing strategies,
   establishing priorities, delegating, sequencing
   and timing, organizing, budgeting, and stan-
   dardizing procedures. People like to have
   order in their lives, and they look to you, as
   their leader, to keep them informed in order to
   insure success. (This area will be discussed
   later in "Leadership: How To . . .".)

4. *Use of Available Systems:* This literally means
   that you understand how to use computers and
   any new technology that will help you obtain
   information to accomplish your mission.

5. *Professional Ethics:* This relates to your
   responsibility to behave in a manner so you

will be a good example to your people.

6. *Communication:* This is the exchange of information from one person to another. (This area is discussed previously in "Factors of Leadership" and later in "Leadership: How To . . .".)

7. *Supervision:* You must control, direct, evaluate, coordinate, and plan the efforts of your people to ensure the mission is accomplished. Supervision lets you know if your orders are understood and shows your people that you are interested in them and the mission. Whatever you do, don't oversupervise. Oversupervision—often called *micromanagement*—causes resentment, and undersupervision causes frustration. You have to have a balance in supervision.

8. *Teaching and Counseling:* This refers to improving performance by overcoming problems, increasing knowledge, and gaining new perspectives and skills. (This area will also be discussed in "Leadership: How To . . .".)

9. *Team Development:* You must create a strong bond between you and your people so that the organization functions as a team. There are three stages of team develop-

There are three stages of team development. They are Formation, Development, and Sustainment.

30

ment. They are *Formation*, *Development*, and *Sustainment*. Each stage presents different challenges.

In the *Formation* stage, people are faced with belonging and acceptance, settling personal and family concerns, and learning about the leader and other people.

In the *Development* stage, they are concerned with trusting the leaders and other people, finding close friends, deciding who is in charge, accepting the way things are, adjusting to feelings about how things ought to be done, and overcoming family/organizational conflicts.

In the *Sustainment* stage, the last stage, a person trusts others, shares ideas and feelings freely, assists other members of the team, sustains trust and confidence, shares missions and values and shows feeling of pride in the organization, assists new members to the organization, and copes with personal and family problems on his own.

Technical competencies are the functions that all leaders must perform if an organization is to operate effectively.

TEACH SUBORDINATES

A leader must move beyond managing programs or directing operations. Leaders must take the time to share with subordinates the benefits of experience and expertise. I suggest that you read T. F. Tenney's *Some Things I Wish I'd Known* and then share with those under you some things that you have experienced. Even the Bible tells us, "One generation shall praise thy works to another, and shall declare thy mighty acts" (Psalm 145:4).

Jesus taught the twelve disciples in order to prepare them for the time when He would no longer be with them in the flesh, not for the time He was still present with them.

When a leader is willing to sit down and share experiences with others, he not only passes on information, but he builds a sense of trust and respect in those under him. Ask yourself, "Who would assume the responsibility of the work I have begun if I were to die?" Jesus taught the twelve disciples in order to prepare them for the time when He would no longer be with them in the flesh, not for the time He was still present with them. Training and teaching subordinates to assume future responsibilities must be a part of every leader's agenda.

BE A GOOD LISTENER

Leaders must listen to their subordinates and superiors. As a leader, you can help your people solve any problem if you listen. Jesus never turned people away. He always listened to what they had to say first and then gave them a reply. Sad to say, too many leaders want to talk before they listen.

Most people who have a problem don't want you to tell them how to solve the problem; they just want someone to listen. The Bible says, "He that answereth a matter before he heareth it, it is folly and shame unto him" (Proverbs 18:13). And James also said, "Wherefore, my beloved brethren, let every man be swift to hear, slow to speak, slow to wrath" (James 1:19). God gave you two ears and only one mouth. A leader should use them accordingly.

Most people who have a problem don't want you to tell them how to solve the problem; they just want someone to listen.

TREAT PEOPLE WITH DIGNITY AND RESPECT

Leaders must show genuine concern and compassion for those they lead. Prejudice has no place in a leader's heart or the organization. It is also essential that leaders remain sensitive to family members and include them in activities. Respect is a two-way street, and a leader will be given the same level of respect that he shows to others. The saying that in order to earn respect you must first give respect is true. Remember the Golden Rule: "Do unto others, as you would have them do unto you."

STRESS AND ENFORCE THE BASICS

A leader must demonstrate mastery of fundamental skills and must ensure that these are taught to those under him. It is hard to lead if you do not know the basics. One of the first schools the military had me attend was Basic Leadership Training. Its purpose was to teach me, as a junior leader, how to stress and enforce the basics. Every day the instructor would tell us that it was the minor details that would make or break us. In other words, those basic things, if continuously overlooked, would get us killed in combat. The basics are what every member of the organization must be proficient in if the organization is to be effective. When the basics are not stressed and enforced, the possibility of the organization self-destructing becomes more likely.

I am reminded of a story about a pastor who

preached the same message each Sunday. Finally, some members of the congregation came to him to voice their concerns and complaints about the same message being preached each Sunday. When they asked the pastor if he had any other messages that he could preach, he replied, "Yes, I do." The members asked him, "Then why don't you preach some of them?" The pastor replied, "When I see you living this one, I'll be more than happy to preach another one."

Someone said that the letters in the word *Bible* mean *Basic Instructions Before Leaving Earth*. As a leader, you must master the basics. May I suggest the Bible first?

SET THE EXAMPLE

As a leader you must realize that you are on watch twenty-four hours a day, seven days a week. Many call this "24/7."

Your daily actions must reflect a personal and professional example for people to emulate. One of the worst things a leader can do is to tell his people to do something that he would not do himself. If you are a pastor, and you don't pray, don't expect your people to pray. If you don't worship, don't expect your people to worship. If you don't pay tithes, don't expect your people to pay tithes. If you don't teach Bible

Your daily actions must reflect a personal and professional example for people to emulate.

studies, don't expect your people to teach Bible studies. If you've never cleaned bathrooms or cut the lawn, don't expect your people to do it either. There can never be enough said about this area in a leader's life.

The US Army Infantry motto is "Follow Me." In other words, lead from the front.

> The US Army Infantry motto is "Follow Me." In other words, lead from the front.

SET AND ENFORCE STANDARDS

A leader must know and enforce established standards. The most fundamental standard that must be enforced and maintained is discipline. Discipline is no more than doing the right thing when no one is watching you. People must respond to orders and take actions for those things that they know to be right when their leader is away. When the religious leaders asked Jesus if they should pay tribute to Caesar, He simply said, "Render therefore unto Caesar the things which are Caesar's; and unto God the things that are God's" (Matthew 22:21). He didn't change established standards. Never lower your standards. Encourage and motivate people to meet the standards.

LEADERSHIP PROVIDES PURPOSE, DIRECTION, AND MOTIVATION

Everyone wants to know "why?" and "what?" Purpose gives people the reason. It lets them know why they should do certain things under certain circumstances and conditions.

At the First United Pentecostal Church in Okinawa, Japan, our purpose is: "That ye might walk worthy of the Lord unto all pleasing, being fruitful in every good work, and increasing in the knowledge of God" (Colossians 1:10). This clearly gives people the "why" and the "what." They can easily see that they must do everything to please God first, to be fruitful, and to learn about God. This purpose is not hard to learn, and even the smallest child can easily recite it. Leaders should never be afraid to give a purpose for what they are trying to accomplish. Purpose relays your intent to the listener and allows them the time to develop ideals within themselves to support you. Whenever you conduct training for your people, give

37

them a purpose for the subject or lesson being taught. The purpose allows them to focus on the importance of the training. It also helps them relate the training to their personal responsibilities and circumstances and see how it can assist them.

Giving people an understanding of the goals to be accomplished is called direction. Direction gives people a sense of confidence because they know their leadership is focused on what they are doing and where the organization is heading. A leader who does not have a vision or established goals for his organization will soon see deterioration within himself and those under his leadership. When a leader knows where he is heading, he knows how to allocate his resources and time to be effective. Direction also shows people what needs to be accomplished in the organization and allows them to exercise initiative in your absence.

Motivation comes in many ways: awards, public recognition, a pat on the back, letters, phone calls, promotions.

Motivation gives people the will to do everything they are capable of doing. Motivation comes in many ways: awards, public recognition, a pat on the back, letters, phone calls, promotions, etc. Remember how motivated the seventy disciples of Jesus were when they returned and told Him that the devils were subject to them through His name. They realized that they, too, could cast out demons. Mark 16:17-18 is one of many motivational passages in the Scriptures: "And these signs shall follow them that believe; In my name shall they cast out devils; they shall speak with new tongues; they shall take up serpents; and if they drink any deadly thing, it shall not hurt them; they shall lay hands on the sick, and they shall recover." If you can get people to believe in themselves, you will be surprised at what will be accomplished.

As a leader, you must show motivation in your own life. The way you look, act, dress, talk, and carry yourself all display your personal motivation. Having a sense of humor and not taking yourself too seriously can help you in motivating others. When a leader understands the basic human needs and strives to fulfill them in his people, he is a motivator.

ELEMENTS OF PROFESSIONAL ETHICS

o Loyalty

o Duty

o Selfless Service

o Integrity

We hear a lot about ethics these days. Ethics set the moral stage for what you, as a leader, should do. Professional ethics say a lot about who you are as a person.

Loyalty: Loyalty means to be loyal to and supportive of those with and for whom you work. It means to fully stand upon an oath that you take. When I joined the military, I took an oath to support and defend the Constitution of the United States against all enemies, both foreign and domestic. When I became a minister of the gospel of Jesus Christ, I took an oath that I would preach no other gospel.

Duty means accomplishing all assigned tasks to the fullest of your ability.

Jesus tested the loyalty of His disciples when He asked them, "Will ye also go away?" (John 6:67). As leaders, things that happen to us sometimes offend us, but when we are loyal to one another and to our calling, we will forgive and drive on. Usually, the people I find who are disloyal are those bucking for position and self-gain. I want to remind you of one thing: You will reap what you sow. If you are disloyal to others, they will be disloyal to you. If you talk and backstab, others will do the same to you.

Duty: A duty is an obligation to do what should be

done without being told to do so. Duty means accomplishing all assigned tasks to the fullest of your ability. The apostle Paul displayed this element; he said, "I have fought a good fight, I have finished my course, I have kept the faith: henceforth there is laid up for me a crown of righteousness" (II Timothy 4:7-8). Duty requires you to take responsibility for those under you and for your actions.

As a Cub Scout, the first words I learned were, "On my honor, I will do my best to do my duty." In a nutshell, fulfill your obligations.

Selfless Service: Selfless Service is no more than putting others and the work ahead of yourself. You must resist the temptation to put self-gain, personal advantage, and self-interest ahead of what is best for the organization and your people. As a leader you must be the greatest servant in your organization. That means putting others before you.

William Cullen Bryant said, "If anything goes bad, then I did it. If anything goes semi-good, then we did it. If anything goes real good, then you did it." Part of being a humble servant is to put others before you and to let them have the recognition for a job well-done.

As a leader you must be the greatest servant in your organization.

Integrity: Integrity is being upright and honest.

As a leader you must be absolutely sincere, honest, and candid. You must avoid deceptive behavior. Integrity is the basis for the trust and the confidence that must exist among members of the organization. People must see integrity in your personal life, as well as in your professional life. If you compromise your personal integrity, you break the bonds of trust between you, your people, and other leaders. Can God say to Satan, "Have you tried my servant (insert your name)?" Does He know that no matter what comes your way (temptation or defeat) you will hold to your integrity?

ETHICAL RESPONSIBILITIES

o Leaders must be good role models

o Leaders must develop their people
   ethically

o Leaders must avoid putting their
   people into ethical dilemmas

Ethics are the principles or standards that guide you to do the moral and right things that ought to be done. As a leader, you have three general ethical responsibilities:

Be a Good Role Model: Whether you like it or not, leaders are always on display. They live in glass houses. Your actions say much more than your words. People will watch you carefully and imitate your behavior. You must accept the obligation to be a worthy role model and not ignore the impact your behavior will have on others. You must be willing to do anything that you tell your people to do. Leaders must set a good example for others to emulate. Future leaders under you will follow your example; therefore, you must present to them the best you have to offer. Your standards and principles must be one step higher than those you expect of your people. People will usually follow one step behind their leader. This is part of human nature.

Develop Your People Ethically: You develop your people ethically by personal contact and by teaching them how to reason clearly. You must be honest with them and talk them through difficult problems. Help them find solutions to problems when there seems to be no answer. Your goal is to develop a shared ethical perspective so that your people will act properly in the confusion and uncertainty of situations. Unless they have learned how to clearly think through ethical situations, they may not have the moral strength to do what is right.

Peter asked Ananias and Sapphira why they lied to the Holy Spirit and kept back a part of the price of their land (Acts 5:3). After their death, the Bible says that great fear came upon the church. I'm obviously not saying that someone has to die to get the point across, but the people you lead must understand that honesty is the rule.

Avoid Creating Ethical Dilemmas for Your People: Since your people will want to please you, do not ask them to do things that will cause them to be unethical. Here are some statements and situations that can give a double message to those you lead:
- "I don't care how you get it done, just do it!"
- "There is no excuse for failure."
- Telling your superiors what they want to hear, regardless of the facts/truth.
- Making reports say what your leaders want them to say.
- Setting goals that are impossible to reach.

Here are a few principles from Abraham Lincoln about ethics:

- Give your people a fair chance with equal freedom and opportunity for success.
- When you make it to the top, turn and reach down for the person behind you.
- You must set and respond to fundamental goals and values that move your followers.
- You must be consistently fair and decent in both the business and the personal side of life.
- Stand with anybody who stands for right. Stand with him while he is right and part with him when he goes wrong.
- It is your duty to advance the aims of the organization and also to help those who serve it.
- If you once forfeit the confidence of your fellow citizens, you can never regain their respect and esteem.

Remember, honesty and integrity are not only the best policy; they are the only policy for a good leader.

LEADERSHIP VALUES

o Courage

o Candor

o Competence

o Commitment

Values are attitudes about the worth or importance of people, concepts, or things to you. Values influence behavior because you use them to decide between alternatives. Your values will influence your priorities. Strong values are what you put first, defend most, and want least to give up.

Courage: Courage comes in two forms: physical and moral. Physical courage is overcoming fears of bodily harm and doing your duty. Moral courage is overcoming the fear of things not involving bodily harm, while doing what ought to be done. It is the courage to stand firm on your values, your principles, and knowing that the required actions may not be desired. There may be times when honestly stating your true beliefs to your superior or to a group may not be in your best interest. It may hurt your chances for promotion or even label you as a troublemaker. These are times that test whether or not you have moral courage to "stand up and be counted." Jesus said, "Fear not them which kill the body, but are not able to kill the soul: but rather fear him which is able to destroy both soul and body in hell" (Matthew 10:28). Have the moral courage to stand for your personal convictions and beliefs, and God will bless you.

Candor: Candor is being frank, open, honest, and sincere with people, superiors and peers and those you lead. In other words, you say what you mean and mean what you say. It is an expression of personal integrity.

Competence: Being competent is acquiring proficiency in required knowledge, judgment, and skill. Competency builds confidence in yourself and your organization. It should be every leader's watchword.

Commitment: Commitment simply means having the dedication to carry out all the duties that you have vowed to do. The apostle Paul stated, "Brethren, I count not myself to have apprehended: but this one thing I do, forgetting those things which are behind, and reaching forth unto those things which are before, I press toward the mark for the prize of the high calling of God in Christ Jesus" (Philippians 3:13-14). As a leader, don't live in the past. Look forward and commit your efforts to the goals ahead. Then lead others toward meeting those goals.

TRAITS OF CHARACTER

- o Integrity
- o Maturity
- o Will
- o Self-Discipline
- o Flexibility
- o Confidence
- o Endurance
- o Decisiveness
- o Calmness under
  Stress

- o Initiative
- o Justice
- o Self-Improvement
- o Assertiveness
- o Empathy or
  Compassion
- o Sense of Humor
- o Creativity
- o Bearing
- o Humility
- o Tact

A *trait* is a distinguishing quality or characteristic of a person. *Character* is defined as the sum total of an individual's personality traits and the link between a person's values and his behavior. Your character is the combination of personality traits that allow you to behave consistently according to your values, regardless of the circumstances. A person's visible behavior is an indication of his character.

The strength of your character as a leader is based on:

- Absence of character flaws, such as indecision, deceit, cowardice, and selfishness.
- Your self-discipline and will to follow your values and beliefs; your strength to be your own person.

As stated earlier, values, such as candor, courage, competence, and commitment, are crucial for all leaders. Positive character traits are also important in a leader. There are no formulas that show which traits are more important than others and how to apply them. As a leader, you need to develop them in yourself and then in your people.

Integrity is utter sincerity, honesty, and candor. It is the avoidance of any kind of deceptive, shallow, or self-serving behavior. Job's wife said to him: "Dost thou still retain thine integrity? curse God, and die" (Job 2:9). Apparently Job was an upright and honest man. He didn't allow his situation to alter his character. He held on to his integrity when everyone and everything was against him.

Maturity refers to the sense of responsibility a person has developed. We must notice the instructions the Lord gave to Samuel when he was sent to anoint David as king: "But the LORD said unto Samuel, Look not on his countenance, or on the height of his stature; because I have refused him: for the LORD seeth not as man seeth; for man looketh on the outward appearance, but the LORD looketh on the heart" (I Samuel 16:7). David must have matured more than his brothers for the Lord to choose him. Our maturity is based on our inward traits, not our chronological age. A leader must have strong moral convictions and values in order to lead others.

The instructions given by the apostles for selecting elders in Acts 6 are a good description of maturity: The elders were to be "men of honest report, full of the Holy Ghost and wisdom."

Will is the perseverance to accomplish a goal, regardless of seemingly insurmountable obstacles. Both Nehemiah in the reconstruction of the wall of Jerusalem and the Hebrew young men in Babylon displayed this trait. Even though their motives were different, each of them had a goal that they desired to accomplish, no matter the obstacles. They were committed to accomplishing the goal before them.

Self-discipline is forcing yourself to do your duty, regardless of how tired or unwilling you may be. Disciplining yourself can **It is much** sometimes be very challenging. It is much easier to discipline others **easier to** than yourself. Our fasting, prayer life, and church attendance are **discipline others** examples of our self-discipline.

than yourself. *Flexibility* is the capability to make timely and appropriate changes in thinking, plans, or methods when you see, or when others convince you, that there is a better way. The apostle Paul displayed this trait when he obeyed the Holy Spirit, Who had commanded him to go into Macedonia rather than to go and preach the Word in Asia (Acts 16). Who can lead us better than the Holy Spirit?

Confidence is being assured that you will be successful in whatever you do. Confidence shows in your bearing, in the look in your eyes, in the tone of your voice, in your enthusiasm, in what you say, and in what you do. The apostle Paul said, "I can do all things through Christ which strengtheneth me" (Philippians 4:13). Just reading this scripture builds confidence within me. A good leader is confident that there will be success in the job at hand. If he is not enthusiastic, his people will lack the enthusiasm and confidence to achieve.

Endurance includes physical, mental, and spiritual stamina. It is the ability to keep going under stressful conditions. Paul said, "Brethren, I count not myself to have apprehended: but this one thing I do, forgetting those things which are behind, and reaching forth unto those things which are before, I press toward the mark for the prize of the high calling of God in Christ Jesus" (Philippians 3:13-14). A leader must take care of himself physically to meet the challenges of day-to-day life. Exercise helps reduce stress and gives stamina to go the distance. I know many leaders don't take the time for regular exercise, but without retaining physical health, you are not going to be able to lead for long in stressful and difficult situations. Walking, jogging, riding a bike, or swimming can all help burn off calories, reduce stress, and give a more professional physical appearance. A leader must have a strong prayer life and must spend much time in the Word to keep his mind focused and to be strong spiritually. Take time for yourself, as the leader, so that you have the stamina to lead others.

Decisiveness is the ability to use sound judgment to make good decisions at the right time. Consider what Ruth said to Naomi: "Intreat me not to leave thee, or to return from following after thee: for whither thou goest, I will go; and where thou lodgest, I will lodge: thy people shall be my people, and thy God my God: where thou diest, will I die, and there will I be buried: the LORD do so to me, and more also,

57

if ought but death part thee and me" (Ruth 1:16-17). Ruth used sound judgment, and we know that she made a very good decision.

Calmness under stress is maintaining a confident calmness in looks and behavior. A leader who cannot handle stress has not mastered this trait of self-discipline. The key to combating stress is rest and planning. Even in a stressful situation, you must still realize that "greater is he that is in you, than he that is in the world" (I John 4:4). You must still look and act like a leader. Remember, people want to follow those who are confident within themselves. If you cannot handle stress, your people will lose confidence in you and will look for someone else who shows confidence to lead them.

A good leader sees things that need to be done and does them. This is initiative.

Initiative is taking action in the absence of orders. Sometimes orders will not be available to you as a leader, and you will have to make decisions. This is where initiative takes place. Never feel that you have to wait for the boss to tell you what needs to be accomplished. A good leader sees things that need to be done and does them.

Justice is fair treatment of all people, regardless of race, religion, color, sex, age, or national origin. Prejudice is the enemy of justice and goes against the Word of God, which is the ultimate Judge. James said, "If ye fulfil the royal law according to the scripture, Thou shalt love thy neighbour as thyself, ye do well: but if ye have respect to persons, ye commit sin, and are convinced of the law as transgressors" (James 2:8-9). As a leader you must treat people the way you desire to be treated.

> **Prejudice is the enemy of justice and goes against the Word of God, which is the ultimate Judge.**

Self-improvement is accomplished by reading, studying, seeking responsibility, and working hard to strengthen your beliefs, values, ethics, character, knowledge, and skills. Remember what Lincoln said: "A good leader never stops learning." When a leader knows his weaknesses, he can use his strengths to help improve his weaknesses. This is all part of self-improvement.

Assertiveness is taking charge when necessary, making your ideas known, helping to define the problem, and getting others to do the right thing to solve the problem. In I Kings 3, King Solomon was asked to make a decision about a dispute over a baby. Not only was he wise in the decision-making process, but he was also assertive in getting the women to do the right thing.

Never think your opinion and ideas don't count. Part of being assertive is knowing when to take action if you disagree with something that goes against your convictions. When there is a problem in the organization, you must help identify the problem and provide input for corrective action.

Empathy, or compassion, is being sensitive to the feelings, values, interests, and well-being of others. It includes making suggestions that help people with problems. "When [Jesus] saw the multitudes he was moved with compassion on them." Let us, as leaders, follow Christ's example. We need to have compassion and understanding for those we are leading.

Sense of humor is not taking yourself too seriously and contributing to the laughter and morale of the people around you. A sense of humor eases tension, combats fear and depression, and enhances communication, trust, and respect. Abraham Lincoln stated, "Humor is a major component of your ability to persuade people."

Creativity is thinking of new goals, ideas, programs, and solutions to problems. Every leader should want to see his people and organization do better. A good leader encourages creativity among *The Led*.

Bearing is shown by posture, overall appearance, and manner of physical movement. Bearing is an outward display to others of the state of your inner feelings, fears, and overall confidence.

Humility is admitting weaknesses or imperfections in your character, knowledge, and skills. Humility is acknowledging mistakes and taking the appropriate action to correct them. James said, "Humble yourselves in the sight of the Lord, and he shall lift you up" (James 4:10). Humility is the opposite of pride.

Tact is a sensitive perception of people, values, feelings, and views, which allows positive interaction. There is a story of a first sergeant (the senior enlisted member of a company) who went out to formation one morning. He told Private Jones, "Your mother is dead." The commander, who was in the back of the formation, called the first sergeant aside and told him not to be so blunt—that he needed to use tact and consider his soldiers' feelings. Unfortunately, the next morning they had a report that Private Smith's father had died. The first sergeant went out to formation and, wanting to use his newly found tact, said,

"Everyone who has a father alive take one step forward." As all the men started to step forward, he quickly added, "Not so fast, Smith."

These character traits are like a tree, and reputation is its shadow. The shadow is what we think of it; the tree is the real thing.

Remember that there is no formula that shows which traits are more important or how you should apply them. As a leader you must develop your own balance of these traits in yourself and in your people.

PRINCIPLES OF LEADERSHIP

o Know yourself and seek self-improvement
o Be technically proficient
o Seek responsibility and take responsibility for your actions
o Make sound and timely decisions
o Set the example
o Know your people and look out for their well-being
o Keep your people informed
o Develop a sense of responsibility in your people
o Build the team
o Don't take on more than you can handle

The principles of leadership are a set of guidelines that you can use to assess your leadership abilities and to develop a plan to improve yourself so you can help develop those under you.

When we think of principles, we think of basics. They are those things that are required of you as a leader to be successful in leading others. Let's take a look at each:

Know yourself and seek self-improvement: To know yourself, you have to know who you are and what your strengths and weaknesses are. When you know who you are, it allows you to take advantage of your strengths and work to improve your weaknesses. Seeking self-improvement means to continually develop your strengths and to work on any weaknesses you have. This will increase your competency and the confidence your people have in your ability to get things done.

Be technically proficient: As a leader, you must study to know your job. Understand how to plan, budget, requisition, and use available systems of technology. This is enhanced when you know yourself and your limitations.

Seek responsibility and take responsibility for your actions: Leading always involves responsibility. Those who do not want responsibility should not become leaders. If you choose to become a leader, then you must seek out responsibility and take responsibility for any decisions that you make while you are in the leadership position. Don't point the finger at others for failures. As President Truman said, "The buck stops here."

Make sound and timely decisions: As a leader, you must be able to assess situations and make timely decisions. Situations that require timely decisions, but are delayed, can have a major impact on the organization or someone's life.

Set the example: As stated earlier, you must be a role model. People look to you to do the right thing and to show them the correct way. It's one thing to tell people what to do; it's another thing to show them how to do it. A picture is worth a thousand words.

Know your people and look out for their well-being: You must know and care about your people. It is not just enough to know their names; you should know some things about their livelihood, family situations, their likes and dislikes. They must see that you care about them and their loved ones. They must see that you are willing to stand with them in the bad times as well as the good times.

Keep your people informed: Keeping people informed helps them to make decisions, execute plans within your intent, and take initiative; it also helps to improve teamwork and to enhance morale. People like to know what's going on.

Develop a sense of responsibility in your people: Leaders who will not delegate authority to their people will never see people who feel they are a part of the organization. Leaders must give people things to do and then let them do it their own way. General George S. Patton said, "Never tell people how to do things. Tell them what needs to be done, and they will surprise you with their ingenuity."

Build the team: As a leader you must develop a team spirit within your people. They must not be allowed to operate independently. As the apostle Paul stated, "Now are they many members, yet but one body." You only become a team when your people trust and respect you and each other as fellow members and when they see the importance of their contribution to the overall organization. As stated earlier, team development is essential in every organization.

Don't take on more than you can handle: Some leaders do not know how to say no. They feel that their boss will see them as failures if they say that they are unable to take on another task or assume more responsibility. Even Jesus asked the question, "Or what king, going to make war against another king, sitteth not down first, and consulteth whether he be able with ten thousand to meet him that cometh against him with twenty thousand?" (Luke 14:31). In other words, you need to consider the cost. Trying to do more with less will only create frustration and will cause your people to quit.

The principles of leadership will help you to accomplish your mission and to care for your people. They are the foundation for leadership. Like the traits of character, there is no formula that shows which principle is more important or how you should apply them. As a leader you must develop a balance of these principles in yourself and in your people.

LEADERSHIP: HOW TO . . .

A leader's job is not easy. You must be able to access every area in your organization to ensure things are being done correctly and that those who are going beyond the call of duty are recognized for their efforts.

Effective communication, counseling, listening, planning, and motivation are only a few of the things that you will have to do as a leader. Knowing how to do things as a leader can make your day-to-day duties less stressful.

LISTEN

The most effective kind of listening is called *active listening*. It's called this because the listener has to work at listening. When you listen to people carefully, they will talk more carefully and will try to make clear exactly what they are feeling and thinking. The best way to get people to listen to you is to set the example.

When to do it:
Whenever someone else is talking to you.

How to do it:
- Listen for total meaning—both the content of the message and any emotion associated with the message (e.g., anger, fear, or happiness). Listen to both what a person says and how they say it.
- If it looks as though someone is so emotional that they are having trouble communicating with you, then gently tell him or her about it (e.g., "Calm down, so that I can make sure that I understand you").
- Test your understanding of the message. For example, while you're listening, ask yourself, "Could I repeat or restate what they just said?"
- Evaluate yourself while you are listening. If you are getting angry or excited, chances are you are not hearing the other person accurately.

How to know if it's done right:
- You begin to see people listening to you more carefully.
- In situations where you have to pass on infor-

Effective communication, counseling, listening, planning, and motivation are only a few of the things that you will have to do as a leader.

70

mation, you don't overlook points or details.
- People want to talk with you.

COMMUNICATE

Effective communication is an absolute must in a properly functioning organization. In a way, "Leadership = Communication." About eighty percent of a leader's time is spent in some form of communication. The leader must learn how to be an effective communicator so that his messages are clear and concise.

When to do it:
- Whenever you send a message to someone, either speak or write it.

How to do it:
- Make the message as simple as possible. Start with clear, simple statements of purpose. Don't overload the message with unnecessary information. Give the "bottom line" up front, then give details or additional information and sum it up by repeating the "bottom line" again.
- Organize your message in a way that the receiver can easily understand it.
- State the message in the receiver's language. Avoid official "jargon" and long-winded wording.
- Use examples to illustrate any new major point or idea.
- Draw pictures and sketches whenever possible.

71

Remember, a picture is worth a thousand words.
* Repeat the important points in the message at least twice.
* Summarize the major points of the message.
* Ask for feedback from those to whom you send messages.
* If time permits, ask the receiver to repeat back to you what you have stated to them.

How to know when it's done right:
* The receiver gives you feedback that lets you know that they understood the message.
* The receiver behaves in accordance with the intent of the message; you see them doing what you wanted done.

I had a pastor once tell me to act as if Jesus was coming at this minute and to plan as though He's not coming for a hundred years.

PLAN

Leaders at all levels need to plan constantly for the future. The estimation of the situation is the best thinking tool for doing this. I had a pastor once tell me to act as if Jesus was coming at this minute and to plan as though He's not coming for a hundred years.

When to do it:
* You have been given a task or see that something

72

in the organization may need to be changed.

How to do it:
- Determine whether you should develop the plan by yourself or get others involved. Does time permit you to involve others? Do others have the necessary skills and knowledge to assist you?
- List alternatives that you think may accomplish what needs to be done.
- Figure out the essential steps in each alternative.
- Put the steps in proper order.
- Determine when each step has been finished.
- Pay close attention to any of the steps that your experience tells you could go wrong.
- Assume that what can go wrong will go wrong and plan accordingly.
- For each alternative way of getting the job done, develop a backup plan to cover things that could go wrong.

How to know when it's done right:
- There is a reduction in the number of "last-minute" problems confronting your organization.
- You can adjust quickly to changes and errors without getting upset.

MANAGE TIME

Time is the most precious human resource. Once

used, time can never be replaced. An important decision made by leaders involves the use of time. What the leader will do with his time and what his people will do with theirs is an essential decision. This precious resource must not be treated haphazardly or carelessly. Use of time must be carefully planned and managed.

When to do it:
- You notice things are not getting done on time, according to your expectations or the required schedules.
- You end up having to do two or more things at the same time.
- You forget about performing some tasks until you are reminded—usually at the last minute.
- Your people are complaining because things just don't seem organized. There is too much confusion in the organization.

How to do it:
- Use a monthly calendar that gives you room to record scheduled activities daily.
- Keep the calendar updated at all times. When you learn about an important activity, record it on the calendar.
- Start a "Things to Do List." Each time you are told to perform a task or you think of a task to

> Time is the most precious human resource. Once used, time can never be replaced.

74

do, jot it down. After you complete a task, mark it off and record the date and time you completed it.

- Establish time limits for meetings whenever possible.
- At least once a day, review your monthly calendar and your list of things to do. This should normally be done in the morning to prepare you for the day ahead.
- When you have a lot to do in a day, list things in priority and do them in that order.
- Develop a timeline/suspense date for projects or tasks.
- Be prepared and willing to work the amount of time you need to get things done. Plan your day around the activities.

How to know when it's done right:

- All required tasks seem to be completed on time.
- Conflict in your schedule doesn't occur.
- Things seem to run smoothly.
- People aren't surprised when you follow up on a task that they are working on.

> The best way to make sure things are done correctly is to set clear, precise standards.

SET STANDARDS

The best way to make sure things are done correctly is to set clear, precise standards. Establishing

Standard Operating Procedures (SOPs) for projected events will accomplish this. People perform best when they know what is expected of them. The most effective standards are those that are realistic, challenging, specific, measurable, and doable. A leader should never assume that the led already knows the standard.

When to do it:
- Your people seem to be putting in the effort, but the results aren't meeting the standard required for job completion.
- You have a new job, and the standards are unclear or have not already been established.
- People ask a lot of questions or seem confused about expected results.

How to do it:
- Read so you will understand how the standard should be stated.

Don't lower the standard because people don't meet it at first.

- Check to see if there are already clear standards established.
- When standards aren't specific, figure out what they should be.
- Make sure the standard is specific and measurable.
- Communicate the standard to people and show them if possible.
- Check to see if people understand the standard.
- Hold people accountable for the standard.
- Measure performance against the standard and

not against others.
- Don't lower the standard because people don't meet it at first.
- Set intermediate standards that will build on the desired standard.
- After a period of time, re-evaluate standards when they appear to be unrealistic (too easy or too hard).
- Establish Standard Operating Procedures.

How to know when it's done right:
- There are few questions and little confusion about what you expect.
- Your people are self-confident and proud of their work.

PROVIDE FEEDBACK

Leaders must give feedback in order to help people learn and grow to overcome substandard performance. Sometimes when discussing job-related problems, a leader may put a subordinate on the defensive. Typical defensive actions include excuses or emotional reactions. The best way for a leader to avoid this is to focus his feedback on the task and not on the individual.

When to do it:
- At a set time during the year or during a project.
- A person's performance doesn't meet the established standard.

How to do it:
- Focus as much as possible on the person's performance rather than on his personality or attitude.
- When you evaluate a person's performance, always do it against the standard, not against the performance of others.

How to know when it's done right:
- The person can tell you exactly what portion of his performance didn't meet established standards.
- He can tell you why the performance was poor.
- He can tell you how he plans to improve his performance.

> Rewards are one of the most powerful tools available to a leader for motivating people.

REWARD INDIVIDUALS

Rewards are one of the most powerful tools available to a leader for motivating people. Rewards show a person that he has done the right thing. It should be in every leader's heart to motivate people to do the right thing. Don't reward only the best people all the time. Remember you are a team. Everyone can be good, but not everyone can be the best. Therefore, show your good people that you value their performance and efforts, too. Pats on the back or public recognition are examples of rewarding people.

When to do it:
- Your people have met or exceeded standards.

How to do it:
- Make sure that people who receive rewards have met or exceeded standards.
- Select a reward based on the performance.
- Make sure people get the award they deserve. Whenever possible, reward in front of others. This will cause new people to see that you reward performance, and they will be eager to be a part of the team.

How to know when it's done right:
- People try to meet or exceed all standards.
- People take increased pride in accomplishing the task at hand.

COUNSEL

There are three types of counseling. They are Personal, Performance, and Professional. Personal Counseling is used when an individual has a personal problem. It can be such things as a death in the family, indebtedness, depression, etc. These situations could require the leader to use this personal counseling. Performance Counseling is used when individuals fail to meet a duty requirement. It is also used when an individual has exceeded duty requirements.

This type of counseling is used to help motivate individuals to improve duty performance. Professional Counseling is also called "Career Counseling." It is used to set individuals on a career pattern, to help in setting goals, or give a course of action for career enhancement. No matter which type of counseling is used, the leader's role in counseling is to help individuals become more effective. The objective of all counseling sessions is to help people solve their own problems.

The leader's role in counseling is to help individuals become more effective.

When to do it:
- The individual asks you for help or advice.
- The individual's attitude or actions have negatively changed.
- Someone else brings the individual to you for counseling.
- At pre-established times throughout the year.

How to do it:
- Make yourself available. Schedule a time for the individual to come talk with you.
- Don't ignore or joke about the problem. Try to build a reputation of dealing with problems honestly, fairly, and effectively.
- Listen, stay quiet, and let the individual do the talking.

- Take your time and be patient.
- Get the individual to specifically state his problem. Ask him, "Can you tell me more?" Tell him, "I'm not sure that I know what you meant by that" or, "Would you give me an example of that?"
- If you think something can be done about the problem, get the individual to reach an agreement on what he should do. If you don't think anything can be done, be honest and tell the individual.
- Keep on the subject. Don't let the conversation deviate from the problem.
- Make sure the conversation focuses on what the individual wants to talk about. Your own stories probably won't help him much.
- Gather as much information about the individual's problem as you can.
- Don't get mad or argumentative about what he says. Keep listening and let him talk. When a person keeps talking, many times he will come up with his own solution.
- Unless you have the correct answer at hand, don't make an on-the-spot decision. Usually, after he has finished talking, an individual will see what he needs to do about the problem.
- Always set a time for follow-up with the individual.
- If you do provide advice, follow up to ensure that the individual did the things you agreed on.

How to know when it's done right:
- The individual tells you the problem is solved.
- The individual's attitude or actions improve.

MOTIVATE

Motivation is simply the set of needs and wants a person has. These needs and wants cause him to act in a certain way. Essentially, motivation is the underlying basis of what a person thinks and does. People act in their own best interests. Understanding people takes a lot of listening, watching, and thinking. If you do it well, you can motivate.

> Understanding people takes a lot of listening, watching, and thinking.

When to do it:
- At all times.

How to do it:
- Always pay attention to the basic needs of people: food, water, clothing, shelter, social acceptance.
- Talk *with* your people and listen *to* them.
- Identify the things that are important to them; know their needs.
- Evaluate to determine how satisfied your people are with what is being done.
- Set the example in everything you do.

82

- Reward only those who earn it.
- Apply corrective actions when needed.
- Promote good people and recommend good people for higher positions even if you might lose them from your team.

How to know when it's done right:
- A person's behavior changes or continues in a desired direction.
- Happiness and unity are present.
- People are willing to do what you ask them to do in order to accomplish the mission. (Of course, you will only ask them to do what is ethical!)
- The organization is accomplishing its goals and mission.
- Participation by people to accomplish the mission is increased.

These "How To's" of leadership are only a few of the basic things that you will be required to know how to do as a leader. Your knowing how to do these things will enhance the organization's ability to accomplish its mission.

WARFARE

Every leader must prepare himself and his people for warfare. Even in the private sector, businesses are in battle with each other and don't realize the stress that this can place on their employees. The apostle Paul told us to "put on the whole armour of God, that ye may be able to stand" (Ephesians 6:11). Warfare isn't an easy task. People get hurt, wounded, captured, and sometimes even killed. This happens when people are not properly trained or the leader shows no genuine care for the people.

Warfare isn't an easy task. People get hurt, wounded, captured, and sometimes even killed.

Two areas we must consider are *stress* and *fatigue*. That's right, these two things kill or hurt more people than you may realize.

Stress is the body's response to a demand placed on it. The demand may be physical (cold, injury, disease) or mental (fear, conflict, pressure). When we are stressed, fatigue follows. Our bodies and minds can't stand up under pressure for long before we become fatigued. We become worn out either mentally, physically, or emotionally.

All leaders face stress and fatigue. Don't feel you have to hide it. Jesus told His disciples to rest. I have heard some pastors say, "We have been fighting the devil" or "Satan has really been attacking our church and people." If this statement is true, there are probably a lot of cases of battle fatigue. In other words, people are tired and stressed out. They aren't fit for the battle at hand.

> **All leaders face stress and fatigue. Don't feel you have to hide it.**

Some indicators of fatigue are:
- Tension: aches, pains, trembling, and fidgeting
- Jumpiness at sudden sounds and movement
- Cold sweats, dry mouth, pale skin, and blurred vision
- Pounding heart, dizziness, or light-headedness
- Feeling out of breath
- Upset stomach—may vomit
- Diarrhea, constipation, or frequent urination
- Feeling tired or drained; it takes an effort to move

- Distant ("thousand-yard") stare
- Anxiety: keyed up, worried, expecting the worst
- Irritability: swearing, complaining, easily bothered
- Difficulty paying attention and remembering details
- Difficulty speaking, thinking, or communicating
- Trouble sleeping—may be awakened by bad dreams
- Feeling bad about mistakes or things that had to be done; much regret over the past
- Anger
- Feeling let down by leaders or others in the organization
- Beginning to lose confidence in yourself and the organization

TREATING STRESS AND FATIGUE

Here are a few suggestions to combat stress and fatigue:

- *"Seek ye first the kingdom of God, and his righteousness."* Go to God daily in prayer for direction. This will help you in planning and obtaining resources for the mission. Seek Him early in situations; don't wait until you are overwhelmed to cry out for His help and direction.
- *Don't waste time with people who are not*

committed. Often in the secular community, there are people who are not committed to the organization—they are just "in it for the paycheck." Sadly, there are too many so-called Christians who are not committed to the cause. They will complain about everything but will never put forth any effort to help. If a leader is not careful, he can spend too much time with these uncommitted people and thus neglect the committed Christians and the mission. Be ready to work with them when they decide that they want to be committed and assist, but don't spin your wheels and become stressed (and ultimately worn down) by those who are not committed. Every person must choose whom he will serve.

Don't waste time with people who are not committed.

- *Have fun.* As a leader you must love what you do and look for ways to motivate and encourage people. Time for relaxation can do this. Fun time can be things like a ball game, fishing, bowling, hiking, camping, or any of the fun games you played as a kid. Sad to say, too many people are stressed because they don't know how to have a little fun. Don't take everything so seriously.

- *Keep the boss informed.* By keeping those over you informed of potential rough spots in the organization, when a problem arises, it will be a little easier to tell them. As I heard one commander state: "If you don't have a problem in your organization, you are not doing something correct." Every group/organization will have problems. Jesus only had an organization of twelve, and He had problems. It is how we deal with problems that determines our stress level and whether we become battle-fatigued.

- *Take a vacation.* Leaders who feel that their organization will fall apart if they leave or go on vacation have a poor understanding of leadership. General George S. Patton said, "If you think you're indispensable, you ain't." Could you imagine the apostle Paul telling Timothy, "I can't go to Jerusalem because I need to remain here in Ephesus. You aren't capable to do the job"? If the apostle Paul was willing to entrust the church at Ephesus to one of his subordinates, we should be willing to trust others under us.

> General George S. Patton said, "If you think you're indispensable, you ain't."

You must also encourage your people to take vacations. Yes, even your right-hand man must be sent from the battle for a little R&R. Encourage them to plan a vacation each year. This pulls them from the battle and allows them to get needed rest. They will return rested and refreshed, ready to meet new challenges.

- *Develop a suspense file.* A lot of leaders get stressed simply because they wait until the last minute to do things. A suspense file keeps you abreast of reports and other information that your boss needs before the last minute. It usually maintains a continual monthly overview of what your higher headquarters will need from you and gives you sufficient time to get those reports in on time. It will help you see ahead of time those projects or programs that are coming up. Then you will be able to make plans to manage them.

- *Don't hold a meeting longer than an hour.* Long meetings are boring and tie up people from being able to get things done. If you are continually having to hold meetings to get information from others who are in leadership positions under you, fire them. Point blank. This, of course, assumes that you have set up a suspense system already. If you have developed a suspense system and they are still not getting the requested information to you, they are not concerned. You shouldn't be harsh with them; you must, however, take whatever actions are necessary to ensure the success of your organization.

- *Physical Training.* Exercising increases the

blood flow and helps the brain and other parts of the human structure function properly. Go into any US Army organization and check the training schedule. Usually the first thing on the schedule after the first forma-tion of the day is "Physical Training." Remember, exercise helps release stress and helps you maintain a professional look and self-confidence.

Remember, exercise helps release stress and helps you maintain a professional look and self-confidence.

- *Stay abreast of changes.* Changes will come and go. What was done one way before may not be appropri-ate for today. As a leader, you must be flexible and be willing to change if it's better for the organization and the people. The enemy can destroy an organization that is not willing to change. After every train-ing exercise, the military has what is known as "An after action review and lessons learned." In other words, they want to know what went well, what didn't, and why. If you host a conference, ask the people to give you feedback. This will help you in planning the next conference and may even give you ideas on how to make it bet-ter, plus it opens a door to those in your organ-ization who have experience planning and conducting conferences. Be willing to change if it's good for the organization.

- *Keep Jesus first in everything you do.* Isaiah 26:3 says, "Thou wilt keep him in perfect peace, whose mind is stayed on thee: because he trusteth in thee." Often our stress and fatigue come just because we have lost our focus—we don't keep Jesus first.

The intensity of combat is so demanding that even the most fit person can temporarily become unable to function because of stress. As a leader, you must teach your people about stress and look for signs of it in the organization and be aware of the impact it has on the organization. During Vietnam, I observed two key members of our thirty-man platoon lost due to stress and battle fatigue. One was the platoon medic and the other the machine gunner. Stress cannot be taken lightly. Just as your people will watch you closely for signs of panic or loss of confidence, you must watch them for signs of stress and fatigue. When you first see signs of stress and fatigue in a person, you should temporarily remove him from the heat of battle so that he does not become a casualty. Give him some "R & R" time so he can get the renewal he needs to accomplish the mission.

CONCLUSION

Leadership is the art of influencing and directing people in such a way as to gain their willing obedience to accomplish the mission. Leaders are role models, example setters, standard bearers, motivators, and teachers. Leaders lead from the front. They are not followers nor are they dictators, but they are the ones who **Leaders lead from the front.** have a vision and know where the organization is headed. They must realize that their basic responsibilities are to accomplish the mission and to take care of the people that God has entrusted to them. A leader must continually evaluate himself to ensure he is setting a professional example for others and seek self-improvement to better himself. Leaders must look to the future and train others to assume leadership should something happen to the leader. Leaders must be willing to allow others to use their own imagination when working on a job. They must be willing to share their experience and expertise with others.

They must know that a good leader:
- Knows his job and does it well.
- Knows his subordinates' jobs and coaches them to do them better.
- Knows how to get people to work together as a team, how to be a part of the team, and how to lead the team.
- Sets high standards for himself and for other team members.
- Is willing to let subordinates make mistakes and, when they do, picks them up, helps them correct the mistake, and lets them try again.
- Treats people with respect.
- Senses when something is bothering others in the organization.
- Is positive and cheerful about what he and the team are doing.
- Retains a positive outlook.
- Doesn't give up.
- Is tough on himself and others when he needs to be, knowing that the toughness is for a good reason.
- Is sympathetic and compassionate when required.
- Is proud of others in the organization.
- Can spot a "phony" or someone who is not trying and has the courage to confront him.
- Is humble, especially in success. Gives more credit for success to the team than to himself.

Much of what I have written I learned over my twenty-eight-year military career. A lot of it was taught to me at military institutions and through assignments, which afforded me the opportunity for promotion. I would be remiss if I did not give credit to those of the US Army who taught me and allowed me to make mistakes so that some day I would be a good leader. I would like to thank the Lord Jesus for His hand of protection and direction in my life and the pastors the Lord has blessed me with; men of God who mentored me and gave me sound Biblical teachings to build my life on. And last but not least, I want to thank my dear family who has stuck with me during my military career, traveled with me around the globe, and endured the hardships in my absence, and who are now leaders and laborers together with me for Christ Jesus.